OSAKA
THE CITY AT A GLANCE

MECHANICS' INSTITUTE LIBRARY
57 Post Street
San Francisco, CA 94104
(415) 393-0101

Osaka Station
Part of the Osaka/Umeda Station complex
and dating back to 1874, this is the principal
railway terminal in the north of the city, with
links to Kobe and Kyoto. Overhauled in 2011,
it neighbours the Grand Front development.
3-1-3 Umeda

Hilton Plaza
In this chic one-stop mall, browse the Louis
Vuitton store (1F, T 03 3478 2100), whose
facade was designed by architect Kumiko
Inui, and call into B Bar (2F, T 06 6341 2375)
for a post-shopping pick-me-up.
1-8-16 Umeda

Breezé Tower
Dine at Zipangu (T 06 4797 3311) atop this
Christoph Ingenhoven-designed skyscraper
for views as inspiring as the food.
2-4-9 Umeda, T 06 6343 1633

Herbis Plaza
Hirsch Bedner Associates' mixed-use high-
rise redefined the station area in 1997. The 40
storeys above ground include The Ritz-Carlton
(see p017). Its sibling is the 2004 Herbis Ent.
2-5-25 Umeda, T 06 6343 7500

Hanshin Expressway
Ugly but necessary in this densely populated
city, the 240km of expressways constructed
high above ground level help ensure Osaka's
roads are less traffic-clogged and the streets
below more pedestrian-friendly.

Gate Tower Building
The expressway couldn't be built around this
16-floor tower, known locally as the Beehive
and completed in 1992, so it curves straight
through levels five to seven instead. Genius.
5-4-21 Fukushima

SINCE
1854

MECHANICS' INSTITUTE
LIBRARY & CHESS ROOM

57 Post Street, San Francisco, CA 94104
(415) 393-0101

INTRODUCTION
THE CHANGING FACE OF THE URBAN SCENE

Osaka was, long ago and very briefly, the capital of Japan. Most locals are more likely to tell you that it's the birthplace of instant ramen. This is an unsentimental city, driven by commerce, with few landmarks to lure tourists. Consequently, not many visitors take the 13-minute *shinkansen* ride from Kyoto, whose measured elegance offers a dramatic counterpoint to its boisterous neighbour.

They're missing out. Osaka is one of Japan's most vibrant cities. The people are noisy, nosy, warm and entertaining. In Tokyo and Kyoto, people mind their own business. In Osaka, they'll grill you about yours. It's not a glamorous place, and there is no coherent aesthetic. But that has given designers the freedom to play. Pritzker Prize-winners Kenzo Tange and Tadao Ando both grew up here, and Ando in particular has had a say in how the city looks now.

Osaka has been expanding since WWII. Unlike Tokyo, which frequently looks to America for inspiration, it is becoming a world player in a distinctly Japanese way. A hotbed of young talent, the creative scene is promoted in cafés and bookshops, street fashions remain homegrown, and design ventures that began here have tended to stay. A stroll through the unnamed lanes of downtown Horie will tell you all you need to know about Osaka's future: the old men's noodle shops still do a roaring trade, but many cafés, studios and galleries are filled with a new generation of Osakans quietly plotting out the next stage in the life of their city.

ESSENTIAL INFO
FACTS, FIGURES AND USEFUL ADDRESSES

TOURIST OFFICE
Visitors' Information Center
JR Osaka Station
3-1-1 Umeda
www.osaka-info.jp

TRANSPORT
Airport transfer to city centre
The JR Airport Express Haruka connects to
Shin-Osaka; the journey takes 50 minutes
www.westjr.co.jp
Car hire
Hertz
T 07 2456 8790
Taxi
MK Taxi
T 06 6452 4441
Tourist card
A two-day Osaka Unlimited Pass (¥2,700)
grants free travel and entry to museums
www.osaka-info.jp

EMERGENCY SERVICES
Ambulance/Fire
T 119
Police
T 110
24-hour pharmacy
FamilyMart + Kusuri Higuchi Kyobashi
5-1-16 Higashinodamachi
T 06 6882 4193

CONSULATES
British Consulate-General
19F Epson Osaka Building
3-5-1 Bakuro-machi
T 06 6120 5601
www.gov.uk/government/world/japan
US Consulate-General
2-11-5 Nishitenma
T 06 6315 5900
osaka.usconsulate.gov

POSTAL SERVICES
Post office
3-2-4 Umeda
T 06 6347 8097
Shipping
UPS
3-3-16 Ishida
T 06 4395 6707
www.ups.com

BOOKS
**Beyond the Bubble: The New Japanese
Architecture** by Botond Bognar (Phaidon)
Tadao Ando: Complete Works edited by
Francesco Dal Co (Phaidon)

WEBSITES
Architecture
www.japlusu.com
Art/Design
www.digmeout.net
Newspaper
www.japantimes.co.jp

EVENTS
Art Osaka
www.artosaka.jp
Transnational Art
www.soho-art-gallery.com

COST OF LIVING
**Taxi from Kansai International
Airport to city centre**
¥14,000
Cappuccino
¥430
Packet of cigarettes
¥430
Daily newspaper
¥180
Bottle of champagne
¥4,500

915.2183
W215
2019
TRAVEL

DEC 2 4 2015

OSAKA

Population
2.7 million
Currency
Yen
Telephone codes
Japan: 81
Osaka: 06
Local time
GMT +9
Flight time
London: 13 hrs 30 mins

Sapporo

JAPAN
Tokyo
Osaka

Beijing Seoul

Shanghai

AVERAGE TEMPERATURE / °C

40												
30												
20												
10												
00												
-10												
-20	J	F	M	A	M	J	J	A	S	O	N	D

AVERAGE RAINFALL / MM

240												
200												
160												
120												
080												
040												
000	J	F	M	A	M	J	J	A	S	O	N	D

NEIGHBOURHOODS
THE AREAS YOU NEED TO KNOW AND WHY

To help you navigate the city, we've chosen the most interesting districts (see below and the map inside the back cover) and colour-coded our featured venues, according to their location; those venues that are outside these areas are not coloured.

MINAMI

This rapidly evolving district is a creative flashpoint. The broad Mido-suji shopping strip is lined with major brands housed in architecturally interesting buildings. Head for Horie and Minami-Senba, where there are cafés packed with hipsters and young professionals on every corner. Namba Parks (see p057) is an example of how to make a shopping mall work; the Glico Man (see p015) is a lesson in marketing savvy.

KITA

Centred around the northern section of Mido-suji, this neighbourhood is defined by its skyscrapers, restaurants and hotels, such as the classic Ritz-Carlton (see p017), theatres, Osaka Station and underground malls. The Umeda Sky Building (see p014) is a long-standing landmark, and Hankyu Men's (7-10 Kakuda-cho, T 06 6361 1381) a stylish department store. The most recent draw is the 2013 Grand Front development.

NAKANOSHIMA

Its international feel makes Nakanoshima seem part of an entirely different city. Osaka's business centre is peppered with Western-style buildings and large gardens. The National Museum of Art (see p062), designed by Cesar Pelli, is a cultural and architectural highlight, and the Central Public Hall (1-1-27 Nakanoshima), sits on the banks of the Tosabori River. It's a great place for a riverside stroll; stop for coffee at Brooklyn Roasting Company (see p038).

OSAKA CASTLE

Osaka Castle (see p013) marks the point where the city was originally founded, and it is surrounded by parkland dotted with cherry trees that burst into life in spring. The park stretches north to the Hirano River, and on the opposite side of the riverbank are the contemporary skyscrapers of Osaka Business Park. Visit the Cesar Pelli-designed Museum of History (4-1-32 Otemae, T 06 6946 5728).

THE BAY

Once an industrial port, The Bay is being reinvented as an entertainment district, but still has a long way to go. There is much striking public architecture here, including Friedensreich Hundertwasser's Maishima Incineration Plant (see p070), and Osaka Pool (see p090), although most local shops and restaurants are past their prime. Check out the art space CASO (see p028) in a converted warehouse.

TENNOJI

Tourists come to downtown Tennoji to tick off two of its landmarks – Shitennoji Temple (1-11-18 Shitenno-ji), first built in the late 6th century, and local eyesore Tsutenkaku Tower (see p009) – then they quickly head back to more graceful environs. But the area is being regenerated and now boasts Japan's tallest building, Abeno Harukas (see p010). Tennoji Park includes the Municipal Museum of Art (1-82 Chausuyama-cho, T 06 6771 4874).

LANDMARKS
THE SHAPE OF THE CITY SKYLINE

The engine room of Japanese industry during WWII, Osaka was pounded by fire-bombing raids that left its predominantly timber structures incinerated and a good many brick edifices destroyed. But the city was quickly resuscitated after the war, and Osaka soon regained its position as a commercial centre and port. Among the buildings to be reconstructed was Daimaru (1-7-1 Shinsaibashi-suji, T 06 6271 1231), the principal department store. Other landmarks, such as the enormous electronic billboard depicting Glico Man (see p015), symbol of the confectionery firm, and Gaetano Pesce's Organic Building (see p066), play key roles in this maze-like town, often providing visitors with their only reference point when they are trying to find a well-hidden café or temple.

A structure that will never win a beauty prize is the 103m-tall Tsutenkaku Tower (1-18-6 Ebisu-Higashi, T 06 6641 9555), which is used as advertising space by Hitachi. Much easier on the eye is Hiroshi Hara's Umeda Sky Building (see p014). Started in 1988, in the era of Japan's bubble economy when Osaka was awash with cash, this was envisaged as a city in the sky, where high-rises would support a plateau of gardens, retail outlets and walkways. The bubble burst, however, and only two towers linked by a viewing platform were completed. It's an impressive sight nonetheless, and stands as Osaka's first piece of destination architecture.

For full addresses, see Resources.

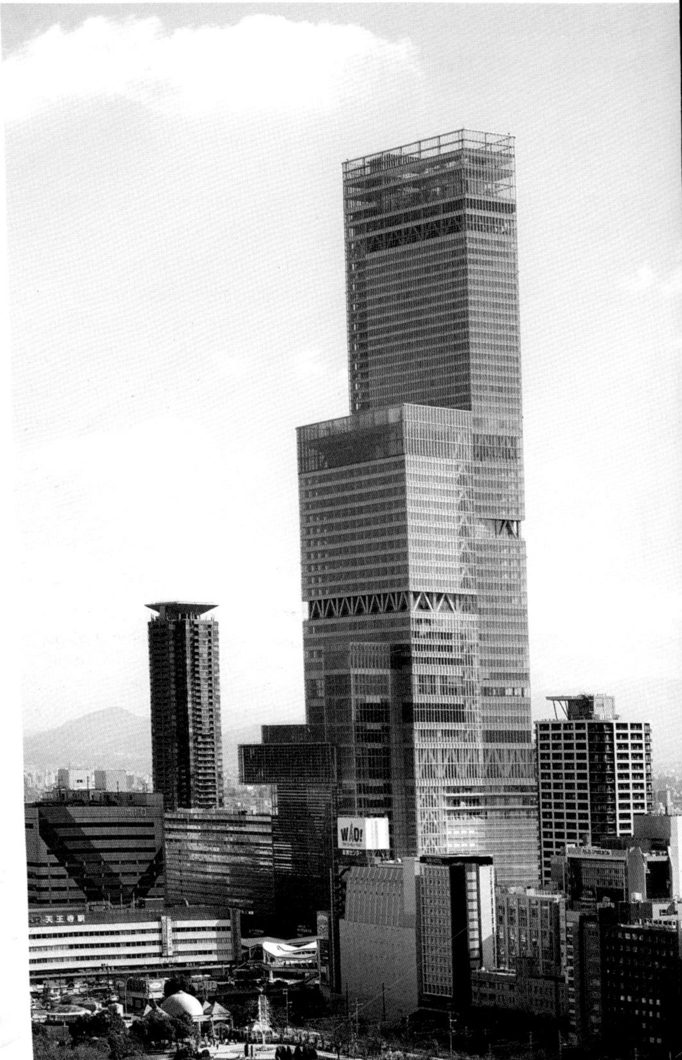
天王寺駅
WAO!

Abeno Harukas

Cesar Pelli has created several of Osaka's
most distinctive structures, including the
National Museum of Art (see p062) and
the Osaka Museum of History (T 06 6946
5728). His most recent contribution to the
cityscape isn't perhaps his best, but it is
the biggest. At 300m, the 2014 Abeno
Harukas skyscraper is currently Japan's
tallest building, exceeding the Landmark
Tower in Yokohama by four metres. The
tiered high-rise, wrapped in glass and
steel, houses a mixed-use complex that
includes a department store, a modern
art museum, a 360-room Marriott hotel
and a two-level Sky Garden observation
deck. The owner of the building is the
railway company Kintetsu. Undoubtedly,
the firm is hoping that Abeno Harukas
does for the dowdy Tennoji district what
Tokyo's Mori Tower did for Roppongi.
1-1-43 Abenosuji,
www.abenoharukas-300.jp

Hep Five

A giant red Ferris wheel atop a 10-storey building may seem a crazy idea, but it's an arresting combination and one of the city's iconic sights. Completed in 1998, Hep Five was designed and built by the Takenaka Corporation, an Osaka-based engineering firm dating back to 1610 that has worked with architects Tadao Ando, Cesar Pelli, Toyo Ito and Herzog & de Meuron. The 15-minute ride, which reaches a height of 106m, starts on the seventh floor and glides past several levels of high-energy retail madness before its air-conditioned gondolas take to the sky. Inside the mall, more than 100 boutiques cater to Osakan teens who have a taste for flamboyant outfits and like to immortalise themselves in the *purikura* booths on the eighth floor. *5-15 Kakuda-cho, T 06 6313 0501, www.hepfive.jp*

Osaka Castle

The depressing truth about Osaka Castle is that it's fake. What's more, the current building, erected in 1931 and renovated in 1997, isn't even a faithful replica of the original 1583 structure. And it's made of concrete. But maybe that's appropriate, as the story of the castle is one of continual destruction and reconstruction. It was expanded between 1620 and 1629; struck by lightning in 1665; razed again in 1868; rebuilt using reinforced concrete in 1931; bombed in WWII; then restored during the late 1990s. Located within a 60,000 sq m site, encompassing the former Osaka City Museum, the castle's seven storeys include displays of samurai armour and weaponry, and a tea room. Big and brash, the landmark embodies the Osakan spirit. *1-1 Osakajo, T 06 6941 3044, www.osakacastle.net*

Umeda Sky Building

This 40-storey building, comprising twin high-rises connected at the top two levels, redefined Osaka and gave it a focal point. Conceived by Hiroshi Hara and completed in 1993, it draws more than half a million people a year to marvel at its implausible design and take in the 360-degree views from its 173m-high rooftop. A postmodern take on the Hanging Gardens of Babylon, it was meant to be surrounded by lush greenery, but planting seems to have stalled at a few trees. Hara believes the towers may yet serve as a starting point for a brand-new layer above the city: a network of elevated public walkways connecting its skyscrapers. For a great view, grab a window seat in the 39th floor café as the sun sets over the Yodo River. *1-1-88 Oyodonaka, T 06 6440 3899, www.skybldg.co.jp*

Glico Man sign

Dotonbori-dori fulfils the fantasies of those who come to Japan seeking the kind of scenes found in *Blade Runner*. At night, the street flickers into life as dozens of illuminated neon billboards, some the size of multistorey buildings, light up. But for Osakans, only one matters: the 20m-tall Glico Man, who appears, arms aloft, over a street-side canal. Erected in 1935, the sign is also known as the '300m runner', after the distance that the calories in one Glico caramel bar can supposedly propel you. At its base is Ebisubashi Bridge, a popular meeting spot for teenage boys and girls, and when local baseball team the Hanshin Tigers win the Central League, it's the place where fans line up to strike Glico Man's victory pose before leaping into the murky waters below.

1 Dotonbori-dori

HOTELS

WHERE TO STAY AND WHICH ROOMS TO BOOK

Osaka has been a trade hub for more than 500 years, yet its hotel scene failed to make the transition from ryokan to Western-style accommodation, leaving imports, such as the Imperial Hotel (1-8-50 Tenmabashi, T 06 6881 1111), The Westin (1-1-20 Oyodonaka, T 06 6440 1111) and The New Otani (1-4-1 Shiromi, T 06 6941 1111) to snap up prime real estate. The big-name global chains can be hit and miss; exceptions are The Ritz-Carlton (opposite) and the St Regis (see p022), although even these can be short on character. Offering a more local experience, the Dojima (see p023) is Osaka's only genuine boutique hotel, while T'Point (see p020) has some of the most eccentric rooms in town. Osaka was the birthplace of the capsule hotel, but it's always had a dearth of attractive budget properties. Addressing that gap are the airline-themed First Cabin (4-2-1 Namba, T 06 6631 8090) and arty Hostel 64 (see p018).

The ambience at a ryokan can be daunting for first-time visitors who don't speak Japanese or who are unfamiliar with Japanese customs, concerning dining or bathing, for example. The Nantenen (158 Amami, Kawachinagano, T 07 2168 8081) is a foreigner-friendly option in the mountains, about 40 minutes from the city by train.

When booking, remember Osakans love to smoke, so ask for a non-smoking room to avoid the smell of tobacco. 'Love hotels' can be good last-minute choices, but often refuse solo or gay visitors. *For full addresses and room rates, see Resources.*

The Ritz-Carlton

You'll find both occidental and oriental touches at The Ritz-Carlton. Paintings and period tapestries adorn the oak-panelled walls, and freshly cut flowers brighten up its antique tables. The 292-room property, which occupies a section of the 40-storey Herbis skyscraper, opened in 1997. As well as the European-style rooms, it offers two elegant Japanese Suites (above). The building is situated just far enough away from other high-rises in the vicinity for each accommodation to afford a splendid panorama, with all the Sky View Deluxe Rooms either looking out towards The Bay or downtown. The most enticing of four in-house dining alternatives is the Michelin-starred French restaurant La Baie, overseen by Christophe Gibert. *2-5-25 Umeda, T 06 6343 7000, www.ritzcarlton.com*

Hostel 64

Until 2010, the design of many of the city's budget hotels was, indeed, cheap. Then, local renovation specialists Arts & Crafts turned a disused edifice in Shinmachi into this cool hostel. The new owners of the 1964 building, formerly dormitory and office space for a machinery manufacturer, retained the most interesting elements, but gave the remainder a ¥30m overhaul, stripping the floors and installing antique joinery and vintage furnishings. Kimono stands have been adapted as coat racks and the chairs come from a bank. In the dorm, *noren* curtains provide a modicum of privacy; the *washitsu*, or Japanese-style, rooms (Superior J-2, opposite) are cosier. There's a small library in the lobby (above), with a selection of design and travel books.
3-11-20 Shinmachi, T 06 6556 6586, www.hostel64.com

T'Point
This quirky hotel's 45 rooms – a sort of ongoing art project – range in price and comfort. Designer Yasutoshi Mifune based the interiors, which are changed regularly, on Balinese resorts, avant-garde ryokans and other styles (Room 614, pictured). Doubles cost almost twice that of singles, but rates include drinks.
1-6-28 Higashi-Shinsaibashi,
T 06 6251 7170, www.tpoint.co.jp

St Regis

The 2010 St Regis significantly raised the luxury bar in Osaka. It secured a key spot on Mido-suji boulevard and an exemption from local building-height limits, resulting in a grand 160-room property with views across the city (from your bath if you're in a Grand Deluxe Premier). The sumptuous-yet-sleek contemporary interiors are by London's GA Design. All the luxe trappings are here: a butler when required; walk-in closets and big bathrooms, standard in all the rooms (Grand Deluxe, above). The 12th-floor St Regis bar is one of the best-looking spaces, its silver-leaf ceiling is one of several nods to feudal-era Japan. Osakan Yasumichi Morita designed the restaurants, including La Veduta, which serves first-rate Italian cuisine.
3-6-12 Honmachi-dori, T 06 6258 3333, www.stregisosaka.co.jp

Dojima Hotel

Akira Gondo of Design Associates Guild and furniture-makers Graf (see p073) teamed up to fit out Osaka's first boutique hotel with pared-down rooms boasting magnolia walls and Brazilian teak furnishings. In the Deluxe Rooms and Junior Suites (above), bi-fold doors, which divide the bedroom and bathroom areas, open to create one space, and make bathing a lot more cosy when shut. A striking charcoal-and-white maisonette-style suite was kept quiet when Dojima launched in 2006, but now pops up on booking websites. Japanese restaurant Hanadori (see p044) is excellent, and even though the ground-floor Diner may not be the social hub it once was, it's still a good place to sit and plan a night out in the nearby bars and bistros of Kita-Shinchi. *2-1-31 Dojimahama, T 06 6341 3000, www.dojima-hotel.com*

24 HOURS

SEE THE BEST OF THE CITY IN JUST ONE DAY

Osaka lacks a tourist trail as such, which gives visitors the chance to do as locals do and get under the skin of the city. You could start the day in one of the cafés in the sprawling labyrinth under Umeda Station, but coffee geeks now have more interesting options, such as Granknot (opposite). Afterwards, peruse the boutiques of the Horie neighbourhood as you make your way to D&Department Project (see po26), where you can browse a selection of covetable wares on the ground level and have lunch on the second floor.

The breezy Bay area provides respite from the inner-city bustle and is the location of CASO (see po28), which offers an insight into the local art scene. On the way back into town, alight at Honmachi Station and stroll down Shinsaibashi-suji, a 600m-long shopping arcade where you'll be fighting for space with the bargain hunters. This strip leads to the Glico Man sign (see po15) and to Dotonbori, where the air is thick with the aroma of street food. Explore the narrow cobbled alley Hozenji Yokocho, an enclave of fine dining, including the *kushikatsu* restaurant Wasabi (see po46).

Come the evening, the Kita-Shinchi district has all the best bars. The sleek Kaara (see po30) is our pick, but there's also Bar Juniper (1-4-4 Dojima, T 06 6348 0414), where you can choose from about 100 varieties of gin, and Elixir K (1-2-9 Dojima, T 06 6345 7890), which has an impressive range of aged liqueurs.
For full addresses, see Resources.

MECHANICS' INSTITUTE LIBRARY
57 Post Street
San Francisco, CA 94104
(415) 393-0101

10.00 Granknot

The baristas behind Granknot, launched in late 2013, learned their trade in an Umeda café, and after reading about Portland's trailblazing Stumptown Roasters decided to create something similar. Design firm Antry devised the branding identity and decked out the interior with reclaimed furniture – the tables are made from wood planks salvaged from a construction site, and the chairs come from a church in the US. Owners Katsuya Shibano and Hideaki Takahashi then added their own creative touches, such as the snaking copper pipes used as wall-mounted light fixtures. The pair work with a local roaster to produce a custom coffee blend, brewed using Kono or Hario v60 drippers, or a La Marzocco machine. Their French toast is also a big hit and a fine way to kick off the day.
1-23-4 Kita-Horie, T 06 6531 6020

12.00 D&Department Project

Housed in a former paintbrush factory, D&Department was founded in Tokyo, and has branches across Japan as well as outposts in New York and Seoul. The Osaka store is a relaxed, airy space and a great place to while away a few hours. The ground floor stocks a well-edited range of homewares, and on the next level there's furniture by Hokkaido-born designer Kenmei Nagaoka, as well as a smattering of vintage pieces sourced in Osaka. In the café (opposite), furnished with black leather sofas by Karimoku60, the European-style menu features mostly seasonal, organic dishes. In the vicinity, check out trainer specialist Skit (T 06 6533 0405), Toga (see p076) and graphic design gallery DDD (T 06 6110 4635). *2-9-14 Minami-Horie, T 06 4391 2090, www.d-department.com*

15.00 Contemporary Art Space Osaka
When container shipping killed off the demand for warehousing, the Sumitomo Warehouse company converted one of its vast units into Contemporary Art Space Osaka (CASO), also known as Kaigandori Gallery. Exhibition quality varies but, due to the 700 sq m of floor space and 6m-high ceilings, it's ideal for big installations. (Junya Komai's 'Art Shower', pictured.)
2-7-23 Kaigan-dori, T 06 6576 3633

21.00 Kaara
This chic, counter-only bar is designed
to evoke a sunset, a soft glow bouncing
off the *washi* ceiling. Veteran mixologist
Koukichi Takahashi has a golden touch
too, serving impeccable cocktails in
antique glasses. Owner Yoshifumi Mori
also runs Michelin-starred restaurant
Kahala (T 06 6345 6778) nearby.
6F Green Terrace Building, 1-1-18
Sonezaki-shinchi, T 06 6341 2818

URBAN LIFE

CAFÉS, RESTAURANTS, BARS AND NIGHTCLUBS

Osakans have coined a word to illustrate their attitude to food: *kuidaore*, which translates roughly as 'eat until you drop'. Proud epicureans, they use it to distinguish themselves from their Kyoto neighbours (more obsessed with clothing) and their Tokyo rivals.

The stereotype of Osaka is of a city filled with cheap, frenetic restaurants firing out local specialities such as *takoyaki* (octopus dumplings), *okonomiyaki* (an egg-and-flour pancake topped with meat and vegetables), *kushikatsu* (cutlets on a bamboo skewer) and udon noodles. It's true that you won't have to go far to find these establishments, but the dining scene is more sophisticated than this. Between midday and 1pm on weekdays, office workers descend on the best venues; arrive after the crush to get a seat. Not all the top-tier restaurants open for lunch, but those that do usually offer their signature fare for bargain prices.

The coffee boom has been a long time coming to Osaka. Hole-in-the-wall caffeine and hot-dog vendor Mill Pour (3-6-1 Minami-Senba, T 06 6241 1339) is a great option in the centre; Brooklyn Roasting Company (see p038) made an impact in 2013 due to its riverside location; and Granknot (see p025) arrived later that year in Horie. Nightlife in Osaka is flash and brash, and Shinsaibashi is the area in which to drink. International DJs don't always head past Tokyo, but when they do, they play at Live & Bar 11 (see p050). *For full addresses, see Resources.*

Mochisho Shizuku

Osaka's most elegant confectionery store specialises in *daifuku* – balls of sticky rice containing bean paste, chestnuts or fruit. Confectioner Yoshihiro Ishida doesn't use artificial additives and makes everything from scratch each morning. He begins work before dawn, pounding rice with a large mortar and mallet, then rolling seven kinds of *daifuku* and shipping them to his three stores in Osaka. Two branches have an old-fashioned decor, but the most recent is radically different. Teruhiro Yanagihara of design studio Isolation Unit (see p084 and p089), conceived the minimalist, all-concrete interior. An 8m-long counter has sweets at one end and seats customers at the other. By early afternoon, the most popular *daifuku* have usually sold out.
1-17-17 Shinmachi, T 06 6536 0805, www.nichigetsumochi.jp

Fukura Suzume
Call it a bakery with a tea ceremony. Or a tearoom with bread. Either way, Fukura Suzume is a brilliant concept. In 2010, husband and wife Masami and Takeshi Tokunaga gave a former grocery store a traditional refit with textured stucco and *washi* walls. The flavours of the baked goods are typically Japanese, featuring ingredients like *hijiki*, sesame and *shiso*.
8-5 Abeno Motomachi, T 06 7504 6419

Millibar

Just a short walk from the boutiques and bars of Minami-Senba and set on a broad backstreet, Millibar feels far removed from the hustle and bustle. The Mediterranean menu, served in the evening, focuses on local, organic, seasonal ingredients and includes tapas and plates of serrano ham. At lunchtime, it's a simpler affair, offering dishes such as pasta, curry and quiche. Between 3pm and 6pm, the stripped-down space is one of the more laidback venues in town; relax in the café area and enjoy a coffee, head to the bar at the back of the room for something a bit stronger or wander upstairs to view the small gallery (above), which puts on contemporary art exhibitions and hosts events for local musicians and creatives.

Artniks Building, 1-12-17 Itachibori,
T 06 6531 7811, www.artniks.jp/millibar

おすすめ

冷茶
煎茶

冷茶黄金桂 五二〇円
岩茶水金亀 五五五円
中国緑茶径山茶八四〇円
鳳凰単欉楊柳葉二六〇円

Tarmerry

Naoko and Koichi Kimura know their tea, and Tarmerry, which they opened in 2008, is all about sharing that knowledge. Their tearoom, on the ground floor of a wooden townhouse, is an unfussy space furnished with three large cedar tables. The main appeal is Tarmerry's selection of Japanese green teas, some of which are aged for 10 years, including the *sencha*, *matcha* and *gyokuro*. There are varieties from the Uji and Asamiya regions not far from Osaka that are renowned for their tea-growing. Order some Uji Watsuka or Uji Watsuka Mukashifu, which are served in earthen pots. These are made from recently picked leaves, and have a sweet yet astringent taste; you can eat the leaves too. Take your time – Tarmerry is all about slowing down and savouring the exceptional tea.
2-4-2 Saiwai-cho, T 06 6567 1130

Brooklyn Roasting Company

This New York chain gave the local coffee scene a shot in the arm with its Fairtrade, organic and Rainforest Alliance roasts, sourced from Indonesia, east Africa and Latin America. Following in the footsteps of its sister branches in Brooklyn, the interior is urban-industrial: bare concrete walls and floors, factory lamps and tan leather sofas form the backdrop for the hip staff in woolly hats working cafetières and a Synesso machine. The range of tasty snacks and small selection of magazines encourage the chilled-out, laptop-toting clientele to linger; wi-fi and power sockets make this a good place to work. The best seats are on the riverside deck (above), which overlooks the Tosabori River and Central Public Hall, completed in 1918.
2-1-16 Kitahama, T 06 6125 5740,
www.brooklynroasting.jp

Yoshino Sushi
This culinary institution, in operation since 1841, is the birthplace of Osaka's signature sushi: *hakozushi*, or box sushi. Chef Takuji Hashimoto puts rice into a square cypress-wood box, tops it with an assortment of cooked and cured seafood, then presses down firmly with the lid. The well-trodden ground-floor entrance gives no hint there's a pristine, modern upper floor (pictured).
3-1-14 Awaji-cho, T 06 6231 7181

Café & Books Bibliothèque

No matter how hungry or caffeine-starved you are, Bibliothèque's 1,500 art, design and craft books, chosen by its staff, will catch your eye. Once you have snapped up a primer on the hottest new Japanese photographer, settle in with a snack. The menu is eclectic, featuring a selection of Spanish and Italian dishes like porcini mushroom lasagne, Spanish omelette, and prawns and broccoli in garlic; drinks include *matcha au lait* (green tea latte) and seasonal specials such as dark cherry mocha and lemonade. Bibliothèque is located in the basement of E-ma, a mall dedicated to fashion. Beauty & Youth United Arrows (T 06 6341 5351), Journal Standard (T 06 4795 7540) and Ships (T 06 4795 7528) are all worth a browse. *B1F E-ma Building, 1-12-6 Umeda, T 06 4795 7553, www.bibliotheque.ne.jp*

Mole & Hosoi Coffees

Tatsuya Hosoi's coffee shop is set in the basement vault of the Shibakawa Building, which was built in 1927 as office space for the scion of a wealthy trading family, but from 1929 to 1943 became a girls' finishing school. The old classrooms now host some of the city's coolest and smallest shops; check out glassware specialist Ricordo, ceramicist Yumiko Iihoshi, and eyewear maker The Stage (see p078). Hosoi moved here in 2008, and retro-furniture dons Buff Stock Yard gave it a subtle refit, installing a steel counter, leather stools salvaged from a hotel and a custom-built oak chest. It still feels like a vault, because you enter through the original reinforced door. The drip coffee and sandwiches pull in a crowd of unusually silent Osakan scenesters.
3-3-3 Fushimi-machi, T 06 6232 3616, www.mole-and-hosoicoffees.com

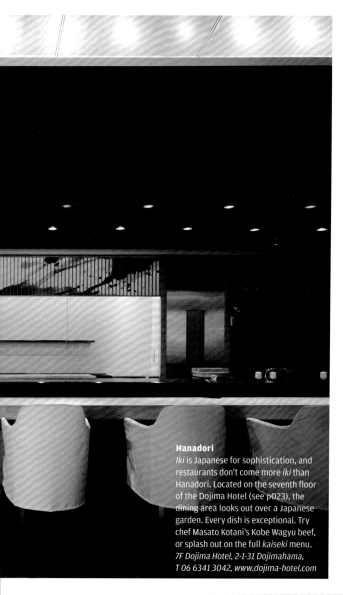

Hanadori

Iki is Japanese for sophistication, and restaurants don't come more *iki* than Hanadori. Located on the seventh floor of the Dojima Hotel (see p023), the dining area looks out over a Japanese garden. Every dish is exceptional. Try chef Masato Kotani's Kobe Wagyu beef, or splash out on the full *kaiseki* menu.
*7F Dojima Hotel, 2-1-31 Dojimahama,
T 06 6341 3042, www.dojima-hotel.com*

Wasabi

One of Osaka's best-known dishes, the cheap-and-cheerful *kushikatsu*, has been elevated to the level of fine dining at chef Takako Imaki's Wasabi. Imaki spent time perfecting her culinary skills in France, and although she says there is nothing French about her food, you don't often see foie gras or frog meat on a *kushikatsu* skewer. Nor do most *kushikatsu* chefs bother to tailor sauces to the ingredients.

There's no menu here: take a seat at the counter and the food will keep coming (and the bill will keep escalating) until you say stop. The creative pairings and elegant modern Japanese interior earned Wasabi a Michelin star in 2014. To experience the other end of the *kushikatsu* spectrum, head to the rough and ready Shinsekai district. *1-1-17 Namba, T 06 6212 6666, www.hozenji-wasabi.jp*

Leach Bar

Osaka business magnate Tamesaburo Yamamoto, a former president of Asahi Beer, bankrolled the construction of the Osaka Royal Hotel in 1965. He wanted a venue that would bring global attention to his city, so developed a concept for its bar with Soetsu Yanagi, founder of Japan's folk art movement, *mingei*. Architect Isoya Yoshida was asked to work on the project and the three came up with the idea of inviting English potter Bernard Leach, a one-time resident of Japan, to collaborate on the interior. Leach used bamboo and brick to create an idealised version of an English country pub, and called on other artisans, such as potter Kanjiro Kawai and textile craftsman Keisuke Serizawa, to help furnish it. The Osaka Royal has since been renamed the Rihga Royal, but that's about all that's changed over the decades.
Rihga Royal Hotel, 5-3-68 Nakanoshima, T 06 6448 1121, www.rihga.com

Live & Bar 11

Osaka's biggest and best club, which is known locally as Onzieme, puts on hip hop, house and techno events for up to 700 clubbers. The boho-luxe interiors contrast with the hands-in-the-air vibe, but this is as sophisticated as young Osaka gets. People come to dance, to show off a bit and make friends. Every tune is lapped up, and the fashion ranges from a carefully chosen T-shirt and jeans to only-in-Japan madness – think Marilyn Manson meets Hello Kitty. On the top floor, there are private rooms overlooking Shinsaibashi, some equipped with karaoke. The likes of DJs Darren Emerson and Soulwax have played here, and the local talent is usually pretty reliable too. Look for Tomoyuki Tanaka or Ko Matsushima on the schedule. *Midosuji Building, 1-4-5 Nishi-Shinsaibashi, T 06 6243 0089, www.onzi-eme.com*

Ambrosia and Sakaisuji Club

Designed by German-trained architect Matakichi Yabe, this imposing, Western-style building was completed in 1931 for the Kawasaki Chochiku Bank. Now, it's the setting for Italian restaurant Ambrosia and Sakaisuji Club, a French eaterie. On the ground floor (above), you can feast on fine Italian cuisine – dishes are both authentic and generous. The large former vaults on the second and third floors are the location of the French restaurant, which offers set-course dinner menus starting at ¥8,400. One vault has been turned into a wine cellar and the old boardrooms are used for private dining. The excellent food and upbeat atmosphere ensure this place is booked up weeks in advance, so reserve a table well ahead.
1-15-12 Minami-Senba, T 06 6265 8000, www.sakaisujiclub.com

Sagan

This riverfront Japanese restaurant is in the basement of the 1926 former HQ of the engineering giant, Obayashi Corporation, and has a striking interior by Tokyo's Atelier G&B. Locals flock here for the tempura and steamed vegetables, and rice cooked in an earthenware pot. It's particularly good value for lunch.
B1 Le Pont De Ciel Building, 6-9 Kitahama-Higashi, T 06 6947 0789

INSIDER'S GUIDE
CHIAKI KOHARA, ILLUSTRATOR

Osaka native Chiaki Kohara is a member of local artists' collective Digmeout Factory. The award-winning illustrator can frequently be found at the associated Digmeout Art & Diner (B1F Arrow Hotel, 2-9-32 Nishi-Shinsaibashi, T 06 6213 1007) located in Amerika Mura, which she admires for the friendly atmosphere and chance to view the work of fellow artists. 'It's a place where creators from all different fields get together and interact,' she says.

Kohara describes Amerika Mura as a hub of the Minami district, packed with cool stores and live music venues. A favourite haunt is the art- and culture-focused Standard Bookstore (2-2-12 Nishi-Shinsaibashi, T 06 6484 2239). She also spends hours browsing Mandarake Grandchaos (2-9-22 Nishi-Shinsaibashi, T 06 6363 7777), which sells new and used anime and manga items. Kohara also suggests visitors look out for the area's street lights, disguised as gangly humanoids. She was one of several artists invited to decorate them. For peace and quiet, Kohara heads to the Tower of the Sun (see p067) or the banks of the Yodo River. 'Osaka is such a bustling, flashy town, but the riverbank is a serene place where I can relax and reflect,' she says. If she is in the north of the city, Kohara will pause for a while in the Toki no Hiroba public space, which connects to Osaka Station's new North Gate complex and plays host to events in summer and illuminations in winter. *For full addresses, see Resources.*

ARCHITOUR
A GUIDE TO OSAKA'S ICONIC BUILDINGS

A relaxed attitude to urban planning has not always served Osaka well, but this hands-off approach has given enlightened CEOs and municipal officials the freedom to commission some exceptional buildings. Cesar Pelli has designed three city landmarks, including the National Museum of Art (see p062), one of his most recognised works, and the high-rise Abeno Harukas (see p010). Friedensreich Hundertwasser turned an incinerator into something resembling a fairground ride (see p070), while Tadao Ando's many buildings scattered across the Osaka area include the Sayamaike Museum (see p060) and Galleria Akka (1-16-20 Higashi-Shinsaibashi). Add to this a growing collection of structures by the current vanguard of Japanese architecture – Hiroshi Hara (see p014), Kengo Kuma (see p058), Jun Aoki and 2013 Pritzker Prize winner Toyo Ito – and you'll appreciate why Osaka's built environment is such a draw.

Investment seems to swing from north to south every couple of decades, and at present the north is rising. The Umeda district around Osaka Station hadn't had a facelift since the bubble era, but railway and construction giants have spent the past 10 years packing the area with multipurpose complexes. Kitahama is the place to view pre-WWII architecture. Here you will see numerous 1920s and 1930s structures, such as the Norin Kaikan building (see p085), which were funded by Osaka's wealthy merchants.
For full addresses, see Resources.

MECHANICS' INSTITUTE LIBRARY
57 Post Street
San Francisco, CA 94104
(415) 393-0101

Namba Parks

Until the 1990s, Namba was the rundown site of an old baseball stadium, and the only reason to visit was Doguya-suji, a shopping strip where chefs still go to buy knives and other kitchen utensils. Today, the area is a real hub and something of an oasis in the fiercely urban city centre. Over a 3.4-hectare tract of land next to Namba train station, Los Angeles-based architects Jerde (part of the team behind Tokyo's Roppongi Hills) created an area of trees, lawns and ponds set around a 30-storey tower and a handful of smaller buildings that house more than 120 retail outlets. To appreciate the architecture, which was completed in 2003, ascend to the Parks Garden urban farm on the ninth floor, where you'll have a bird's-eye view. *2-10-70 Nambanaka, T 06 6644 7100, www.nambaparks.com*

Asahi Broadcasting Corporation

The Osaka-based ABC gave Kengo Kuma an 8,500 sq m riverside plot to utilise for their new HQ. His waterfront design is both dramatic and accessible, as well as sustainable. The chequered facade made from reconstituted timber evokes an old Japanese puzzle box, but it serves a practical purpose too, allowing the river breeze to cool the building in winter and to limit heat absorption in summer. Kuma wanted to create architecture that Osakans could connect with, rather than a secure fortress, so he designed a grand open-air staircase that guides visitors through the heart of the structure and on to a riverside deck. The 300-capacity ABC Hall, which is operated by Asahi, hosts a variety of arts events. The architecture is best viewed from the opposite bank of the Dojima.

1-1-30 Fukushima

Prefectural Sayamaike Museum
Tadao Ando designed this striking complex,
inaugurated in 2001, as a memorial to
the engineers who had brought irrigation
technology to the region more than 1,400
years ago. Given free rein over a 15,400 sq
m site, the architect used cascading water,
concrete and light to create a modern
temple to ancient practices.
2 Ikejirinaka, Osaka Sayama, T 07 2367 8891,
www.sayamaikehaku.osakasayama.osaka.jp

National Museum of Art

Osakans dub it the 'submarine', whereas Argentine-American architect Cesar Pelli, the man responsible for this building's audacious design, calls it a 'bathtub, in a bathtub, in a bathtub'. Either way, when Pelli's splash of steel tubes was erected over the National Museum of Art it made waves. The three-level structure, which opened in 2004, is buried on an island in the centre of the city, and is encased in 10m-thick walls just in case the river should meander in an alternative direction. The permanent exhibition includes works by major figures such as Paul Cézanne, Tsuguharu Fujita and Jasper Johns, and temporary shows, most of which have an Asian theme, are put on throughout the year. Next door is the Science Museum. *4-2-55 Nakanoshima, T 06 6447 4680, www.nmao.go.jp*

National Museum of Ethnology
Known locally as Minpaku, the Museum of Ethnology expresses Kisho Kurokawa's belief that buildings should 'evolve' via alterations and additions. Constructed in the grounds of Osaka Expo Park and opened in 1977, this huge museum has 51,225 sq m of floor space displaying some 10,000 items drawn from a collection of 350,000 artefacts sourced from all over the world. The design is based around a series of 'capsules' – small buildings set in a courtyard that allow for flexibility and expansion. It is a concept that Kurokawa explored for much of his career, and the turrets (overleaf) and bulging, rounded corners are typical of his style. They also presage the shift to more fluid forms that occurred as postmodernism developed.
10-1 Senri Banpaku Koen, Suita,
T 06 6876 2151, www.minpaku.ac.jp

Organic Building

Designer Gaetano Pesce made an impact internationally in 1969 with his Up range of furniture, and has created pieces for B&B Italia, Cassina and Vitra. The New York-based Italian has also designed a sprinkling of enigmatic edifices, the most admired of which is Osaka's 1993 Organic Building. This nine-storey office block, constructed for *konbu* seaweed wholesaler Oguraya Yamamoto, is clad with 132 organically shaped fibreglass funnels that are planted with 80 types of indigenous flora. The year after its completion, city leaders declared the structure a civic landmark, and agreed to take over responsibility for the garden's upkeep. Today, it is a popular reference point, and a building that locals have definitely taken to their hearts.
4-7-21 Minami-Senba

Tower of the Sun

This 70m-high sculpture by Taro Okamoto faces the Expo 1970 Commemorative Park gates, through which more than 64 million visitors passed that year. A former student at the Sorbonne in Paris, where he mixed with the likes of Georges Bataille and Max Ernst, Okamoto occupied an unusual role in Japan – a serious writer and artist, who also appeared as a comic on knockabout TV shows until his death in 1996. *Tower of the Sun* is his most famous work, and one of the few Expo structures that remain; another is Isamu Noguchi's *Moon World*, a cratered sphere that few would guess was by the Japanese-American artist. Today, the park includes the National Museum of Ethnology (see p063) and a walkway weaving through the treetops.

1-1 Senri Banpaku Koen, Suita,
T 06 6877 7387, www.expo70.or.jp

Kansai International Airport Terminal
Perched on an artificial island in Osaka Bay, Renzo Piano's terminal for Kansai International has an elegant, wing-like roof that stretches 1.7km, making it the world's longest airport building. Opened in 1994, the undulating steel-and-glass structure redefined modern airport design. No mere holding pen for weary travellers, this is an audacious space that works efficiently and is easy to navigate.

The airport proved itself in a different way when it withstood the devastating Kobe earthquake of 1995, which struck 20km away. Not one of the grand windows overlooking its aircraft bays was shattered. It also survived a powerful typhoon in 1998. Osaka's other airport, closer to the centre, handles domestic flights only.
1 Senshu-kuko Kita, Izumisano,
T 07 2455 2500, www.kansai-airport.or.jp

Maishima Incineration Plant

Few waste plants attract tourists, but then few have been designed by Friedensreich Hundertwasser, the late Viennese artist. Opened in 2001, this facility was given its dramatic exterior, evoking the flames at its heart, as part of the city's attempt to spruce up its image during a bid to host the 2008 Olympics. Original canvases by Hundertwasser hang on the interior walls.
1-2-48 Hokkoshiratsu, T 06 6463 4153

SHOPPING

THE BEST RETAIL THERAPY AND WHAT TO BUY

Trade defines Osaka. Centuries before Japan opened commercial relations with the West in the mid-19th century, the Sakai area of Osaka Prefecture was selling swords, crafts and copper to China and South-East Asia. And although it's only old men who still greet each other with *Mokarimakka?* ('Have you turned a profit?'), the people here are always devising new products to market. Osaka was the first place to retail calculators, TVs and camera phones.

Over the past decade, developers have been pouring money into multipurpose complexes such as Herbis Plaza (2-5-25 Umeda, T 06 6343 7500), Abeno Harukas (see p010) and Namba Parks (see p057). The most successful has been the vast Grand Front (T 06 6372 6300), completed in 2013 and situated next to Osaka Station. It encompasses a Knowledge Capital area, a diverse space in which companies and researchers show off their visions of the future.

Entrepreneurs have fashioned retail zones by clustering their shops in Horie, Minami-Senba and Kitahama. Mido-suji, Osaka's venerable shopping street, has also been spruced up by branches of Hermès (3-10-25 Minami-Senba, T 06 4704 7110) and Apple (1-5-5 Nishi-Shinsaibashi, T 06 4963 4500). The only obstacle to fruitful shopping is Osaka's baffling address system, in which small streets go unnamed and building numbers need a maths PhD to decipher. Avoid confusion by asking your concierge for a map and directions. *For full addresses, see Resources.*

Graf

In 2000, a product designer, a carpenter, a furniture-maker, a chef, an architect and an artist formed the collective Decorative Mode No 3 to create unique products and reach innovative, interdisciplinary design solutions. Retailing their wares under the brand name Graf, the group manufactures furniture, such as this tamo wood chair (above), ¥153,000, in addition to lighting and kitchenware, occasionally working in collaboration with other firms. They also hold workshops on woodworking and take on interior and graphic design projects. In 2013, the company relocated a few doors down the street to an airy new showroom (overleaf), encompassing a small café that serves drinks and seasonal lunch dishes. It all makes for a win-win combination. *4-1-9 Nakanoshima, T 06 6459 2100, www.graf-d3.com*

Graf

Toga

Costumier-turned-designer Yasuko Furuta won a band of global fans when she first showed in Paris in 2006. Her business now stretches to five Toga shops, including this outlet in Minami (there are also branches in Tokyo and Kanazawa). The Osaka store's urban-industrial interior features select antique furnishings and complements the silhouette of Furuta's edgy yet wearable womenswear, which alludes to classic shapes and is distinctly Japanese without resorting to cliché. There are various Toga lines on sale, including Pulla (daywear); Elastic (lingerie); Picta (jewellery and one-off pieces fashioned from recycled textiles); and Virilis (menswear). Furuta's vintage streetwear finds are displayed on shelves at the back of the store.
1-23-7 Kita-Horie, T 06 6533 7538,
www.toga.jp

Especial Records

The Okino brothers, Shuya and Yoshihiro, who make up the renowned group Kyoto Jazz Massive, are based in Tokyo and Osaka respectively. Whereas Shuya has chosen to add radio DJ and writer to his resumé, Yoshihiro started a record shop and label. As you might expect, this is no ordinary music store. Especial Records looks like a friend's house that just happens to stock some of the best and rarest house, hip hop and nu jazz tracks anywhere in Japan. The place is tiny, but scour the racks and you'll find an obsessively well-chosen collection of new and secondhand vinyl and CDs. When Yoshihiro's in town, he's behind the counter but, if you want to hear him DJ, go to Circus (T 06 6241 3822) or Kyoto, where he's a regular at Metro (T 07 5752 4765).
Sakura Building, 4-9-2 Minami-Senba, T 06 6241 0336, www.especial-records.com

The Stage

The city of Sabae produces 95 per cent of Japan's eyewear, and many of its best craftsmen work for Kaneko Optical. This store, in Osaka's Shibakawa Building, is a tribute to their skills and production techniques. All frames are handmade and stamped with the maker's name. Across the corridor is a mini-museum, dedicated to the history of optometry.
3-3-3 Fushimi-machi, T 06 6204 5280

Truck

It's a bit of a trek out to Truck, and there's little else to see nearby, but it's well worth the effort – this is Osaka's most interesting furniture shop. Husband-and-wife team Tokuhiko Kise and Hiromi Karatsu design the pieces together, then Kise works out how to build them. The duo's creations are characterful but unfussy, and utilise oak, walnut and iron. They have a penchant for what they call 'furrowed leather', made from Japanese hides soaked in tannins to bring out the texture, then softened with fish oils. The products aren't sold in other stores, but can be made to order and shipped. After a look around, head across the street to Bird (above), their hip coffee shop furnished with Truck designs. Closed Tuesdays and some Wednesdays.
6-8-48 Shinmori, T 06 6958 7055,
www.truck-furniture.co.jp

Elttob Tep
This store sells all Issey Miyake's lines,
items by his one-time creative director
Naoki Takizawa, and the work of new
talent. The shop's name, Pet Bottle spelt
backwards, hints at its playfulness.
The space was designed by Taku Satoh,
a director of Miyake's 21_21 Design Sight
in Tokyo. Shelves suspended from the
ceiling allow for a moveable display.
4-11-28 Minami-Senba, T 06 6251 8887

Calo Bookshop & Café

This is an ideal place to find out what's happening in Osaka's creative community. Opened by Akiko Ishikawa in 2004, Calo specialises in titles on visual culture, as well as hard-to-find magazines from around the world. Created by Isolation Unit's Teruhiro Yanagihara, the space is pared down, with angular furnishings set out under a raw concrete ceiling. Wooden benches and bookcases add some warmth to the interior. The café serves an eclectic mix of foreign fare, including Earl Grey tea with scones, and a popular chicken curry with brown rice sourced from Kansai's Shiga Prefecture. Calo also manages a gallery in the same location, in which it displays monthly exhibitions showcasing local artists.

5F Wakasa Building, 1-8-24 Edobori,
T 06 6447 4777, www.calobookshop.com

Norin Kaikan

Once a cheap option for cash-strapped retailers, Osaka's older buildings are now prime real estate. Today, every boutique wants to occupy an early 20th-century property, and the 1930 Norin Kaikan in Minami tops the list. Constructed for the Mitsubishi Corporation, it was sold to a former high-ranking agriculture ministry bureaucrat, who renamed it Norin Kaikan (Agriculture and Forestry Hall) and invited in creative companies looking for pastures new. Explore its corridors and you'll come across the bike shop Tokyo Wheels (T 06 4400 5070); Maison Martin Margiela (T 06 6282 0009); stationery and design bookshop Flannagan (T 06 6120 2416); and Sencha To Kutsushita Soshite Yakuso ('Tea, Socks and Herbal Medicines', T 070 5438 2016), which has a cute tearoom.
2-6-3 Minami-Senba, www.osaka-norin.com

Winged Wheel

It takes a lot for a stationery store to stand out in Japan, but Winged Wheel does so with a combination of fine craftsmanship and quirky designs. The brand is the retail spin-off of Haguruma Envelope, a company that has been manufacturing top-quality stationery since 1918. Its signature high-grade *washi* paper is made from Japanese mulberry trees, but its real speciality is handmade, highly textured cotton paper, produced in a town in the foothills of Mount Fuji. The detail goes well beyond the paper itself: cards are foil-stamped or embossed with traditional Japanese motifs in pop colours, and often finished by hand. Visit on a weekday if you want time to browse, because on weekends Winged Wheel is a magnet for couples shopping, slowly, for wedding stationery. The store can also print business cards and letterheads.
3-6-14 Minami-Senba, T 06 6245 8430, www.winged-wheel.co.jp

SPORTS AND SPAS
WORK OUT, CHILL OUT OR JUST WATCH

Sport in Osaka can be summed up in two words: Hanshin Tigers. The mood of this city rises and falls with the fortunes of its baseball team, who are sponsored by the Hanshin railway company. When the Tigers won the Central League in 2003 and 2005, thousands of ecstatic fans converged on Ebisubashi Bridge (see p015) and made the celebratory jump into the Dotonbori canal. So closely linked are the team and the city that the 2003 win was calculated to have resulted in an economic boom worth almost £2bn. The Tigers' stadium is actually in another city, Nishinomiya, while local also-rans the Orix Buffaloes play in the Osaka Dome. You won't hear them mentioned that much. Football runs a distant second to baseball, but J League team Gamba Osaka still draw passionate crowds of 10,000 to 20,000. They were one of the teams to beat during the noughties, but by 2013 were playing in the second tier.

Runners will find company in the park around Osaka Castle (see p013), or along the Yodo River. Certain fitness centres, such as Nobiyaka Kenkokan (see p092), welcome drop-in visitors, and swimmers can notch up lengths at Osaka Pool (see p090). The biggest annual events here include the Takarazuka Kinen horse race at Hanshin Racecourse (1-1 Komano-cho, Takarazuka, Hyogo) in June, and the Tour of Japan cycle race (www.toj.co.jp) in May, when teams of international riders pedal from Osaka to Tokyo. *For full addresses, see Resources.*

MECHANICS' INSTITUTE LIBRARY
57 Post Street
San Francisco, CA 94104
(415) 393-0101

Ne

Fashionable Horie has plenty of hair salons but none as striking as Ne. Husband-and-wife stylists Minoru Kozaki and Mutsumi Uranaka envisaged their salon as a stage, with their clients as the audience. In 2010, master of minimalism Teruhiro Yanagihara designed their extraordinary theatre. The all-white room looks as if it's constructed from folded paper, the cupboard doors and lampshades resembling cut-out flaps.

Near the entrance, concrete steps serve as the waiting room (and conceal the loo). Cleverly angled mirrors make the room feel spacious and expose the rest of the salon, while focusing the patron's gaze on their stylist. The few furnishings (breeze-block lamp stands, carpenters' benches, steel trolleys) reinforce the aesthetic.
2F 1-13-21 Kita-Horie, T 06 4395 5634, www.ne-hair.com

Osaka Pool
Do several laps of backstroke at this facility, designed by Tohata Architects & Engineers and completed in 1996, to appreciate the stunning, structurally intriguing roof composed of 3,300 sq m of strong, impressively flexible fabric. There are two 50m pools, one of which is converted into an ice rink in winter.
Koen Nai, 3-1-20 Tanaka,
T 06 6571 2010

Nobiyaka Kenkokan

Kisho Kurokawa's 'relaxed health club' is almost too beautiful to raise a sweat in. Taking its inspiration from the waves of nearby Sakai harbour in Osaka Bay, the curved glass building, completed in 2004, seems to melt into the surrounding park. Inside, there's a gym, a 25m pool and a dance studio, in addition to air-conditioned tennis courts and futsal pitches. In an effort to reduce CO_2 emissions, the club uses heat created by a nearby waste incineration plant, as well as recycled rainwater in the bathrooms and gardens. All of the facilities can be used by non-members. The journey on the Nankai line from Namba Station to Sakai, famous for its cutlery industry and ancient burial mounds, takes about 15 minutes.
2760-1 Kanaokacho, Kita-ku, Sakai,
T 07 2246 5051, www.sakaiwellness.com

Nagai Stadium

Open since 1964, the Nagai Stadium has been host to some of the world's biggest sporting events, including the 2007 IAAF World Athletics Championships and three games during the 2002 FIFA World Cup. The venue originally had 23,000 seats, but was knocked down in the early 1990s. It was rebuilt by Osakan architectural firm Showa Sekkei to accommodate 50,000 spectators (who are protected from the elements by two pillarless roofs), and was reopened in 1996. Tickets for local football matches can be bought at the gate. The track is not accessible to casual runners, but a 2.8km course loops right around the venue and through the 67.5-hectare Nagai Park, which was inaugurated in 1959 and includes a raft of recreational facilities. *1-1 Nagai Koen, Higashi-Sumiyoshi-ku, T 06 6691 2500, www.nagai-park.jp*

ESCAPES

WHERE TO GO IF YOU WANT TO LEAVE TOWN

Add up the land mass of the 6,852 islands that form the Japanese archipelago and the total area is still smaller than California. In a nation of 127 million people, this means urban centres are densely packed and personal space is at a premium, but also neighbouring cities are easier to reach than you may think.

If you want to visit Japan's former capitals, board a *shinkansen* and you can be in ancient Kyoto in less than 15 minutes; head west for 25 minutes and you'll reach Kobe, the capital for five months in 1180. Close to here you can rejuvenate at the Negiya Ryofukaku onsen (see p101). Less than an hour east is Nara, where sika deer roam the streets, and the colossal Daibutsu-den, part of the World Heritage-listed Todaiji temple complex, has stood for more than 1,200 years. The buzzy and more modern Fukuoka is an 80-minute flight away; explore Tenjin, which is filled with hip boutiques and restaurants. If you're leaving Osaka from Kansai Airport (see p068), catch the retro-cool Rapi:t express train from Namba Station.

The islands of the Seto Inland Sea are strewn with interesting art venues. Travel to Naoshima via Okayama, then take the ferry across to Inujima (opposite). Architectural highlights include IM Pei's Miho Museum (see p100) in Shiga Prefecture, and Frank Lloyd Wright's Yodoko Guest House (see p102), which you can reach via a journey on the cute Hanshin train from Umeda Station.

For full addresses, see Resources.

Inujima Seirensho Art Museum

The copper refinery on Inujima island was in operation for just 10 years in the early 20th century. It was then left to crumble for nearly nine decades, until businessman Soichiro Fukutake decided to transform it into an art museum. Architect Hiroshi Sambuichi preserved much of the original building, utilising discarded local granite and bricks to reconstruct the interior, allowing for the use of geothermal and solar energy in the design. Yukinori Yanagi provided the art, including an installation that features fragments of author Yukio Mishima's house strung from the ceiling. Elsewhere on the island, visit the Kazuyo Sejima-designed Art House Project (T 08 6947 1112) and Seaside Inujima Gallery (T 08 6947 1112) with works by Fiona Tan. *327-5 Inujima, Higashi-ku, T 08 6947 1112, www.benesse-artsite.jp/seirensho*

Inujima Seirensho Art Museum

Miho Museum

The 1997 Miho Museum is destination architecture, which is just as well, because visiting it entails a pilgrimage by train, bus and foot to the cedar covered mountains of Shiga Prefecture, via Ishiyama. Here, IM Pei created a stunning building constructed of French limestone, concrete, steel and glass. Inside, you can view an impressive collection of international antiquities and art assembled by late textile-firm heiress Mihoko Koyama. Not only did she spend more than ¥30,000m on the museum, Koyama became notorious in Japan for leaving the Church of World Messianity to establish her own religion, Shinji Shumeikai. Opening days vary with the seasons, so make sure you check the website before setting off on your trip. *300 Tashiro Momodani, Shigaraki, Shiga, T 07 4882 3411, www.miho.jp*

Negiya Ryofukaku

The Arima Onsen resort, an hour by train from Osaka, dates back to the 8th century. Feudal ruler Hideyoshi Toyotomi reportedly liked to recuperate here. The 33-room Negiya Ryofukaku ryokan opened in 1857, and its name recalls its original purpose, a rest house for Shinto priests. One reason it has lasted so long is that it has modernised without sacrificing its historic character. As part of a 2010 renovation, design firm Process5 created four new rooms, using maple throughout to reference the trees surrounding the inn. They split each one (Rebirth, above) in two, with a tatami-mat area by the entrance and a Western-style bedroom. Order a traditional ryokan tea or dinner, then lie back on the sofa facing the window and lush Arima scenery.
1537-2 Arima-cho, Kita-ku, Hyogo,
T 07 8904 0675, www.negiya.jp

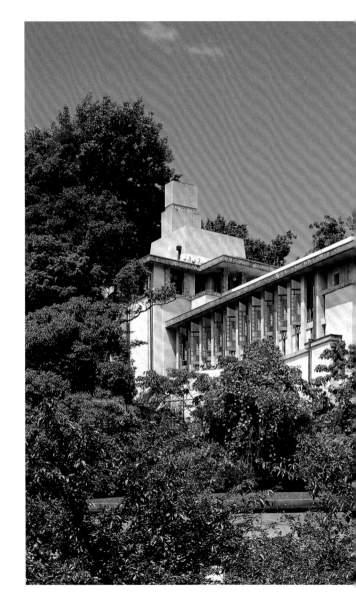

Yodoko Guest House, Ashiya
Frank Lloyd Wright spent seven years in
Japan and this 1924 residential building
is a key part of his legacy. Nestled into
the hillside, its four storeys of volcanic
Oyaishi stone are framed by greenery.
Dozens of small shuttered windows set
high up help control light and ventilation.
Open on Wednesdays and at weekends.
*3-10 Yamanote-cho, Hyogo, T 07 9738
1720, www.yodoko.co.jp/geihinkan*

NOTES

SKETCHES AND MEMOS

RESOURCES
CITY GUIDE DIRECTORY

A

Abeno Harukas 010
1-1-43 Abenosuji
www.abenoharukas-300.jp

Ambrosia 051
1-15-12 Minami-Senba
T 06 6265 8000
www.sakaisujiclub.com

Apple 072
1-5-5 Nishi-Shinsaibashi
T 06 4963 4500
www.apple.com/jp

Art House Project 097
327-5 Inujima
Higashi-ku
Okayama
Inujima
T 08 6947 1112
www.benesse-artsite.jp/inujima-arthouse

Asahi Broadcasting Corporation 058
1-1-30 Fukushima

B

Bar Juniper 024
1-4-4 Dojima
T 06 6348 0414

Beauty & Youth United Arrows 042
B2F E-ma Building
1-12-6 Umeda
T 06 6341 5351
www.beautyandyouth.jp

Brooklyn Roasting Company 038
2-1-16 Kitahama
T 06 6125 5740
www.brooklynroasting.jp

C

Café & Books Bibliothèque 042
B1F E-ma Building
1-12-6 Umeda
T 06 4795 7553
www.bibliotheque.ne.jp

Calo Bookshop & Café 084
5F Wakasa Building
1-8-24 Edobori
T 06 6447 4777
www.calobookshop.com

Circus 077
2F Nakanishi Building
1-8-16 Nishi-Shinsaibashi
T 06 6241 3822
www.circus-osaka.com

Contemporary Art Space Osaka 028
2-7-23 Kaigan-dori
T 06 6576 3633
www.caso-gallery.jp

D

Daimaru 009
1-7-1 Shinsaibashi-suji
T 06 6271 1231
www.daimaru.co.jp/shinsaibashi

D&Department Project 026
2-9-14 Minami-Horie
T 06 4391 2090
www.d-department.com

DDD 037
1F Namba SS Building
1-17-28 Minami-Horie
T 06 6110 4635
www.dnp.co.jp

Digmeout Art & Diner 054
B1F Arrow Hotel
2-9-32 Nishi-Shinsaibashi
T 06 6213 1007
www.digmeoutcafe.com

E
Elixir K 024
1-2-9 Dojima
T 06 6345 7890
Elttob Tep 082
4-11-28 Minami-Senba
T 06 6251 8887
www.elttobtep.com
Especial Records 077
Sakura Building
4-9-2 Minami-Senba
T 06 6241 0336
www.especial-records.com

F
Flannagan 085
Norin Kaikan
2-6-3 Minami-Senba
T 06 6120 2416
www.flannagan.biz
Fukura Suzume 034
8-5 Abeno Motomachi
T 06 7504 6419

G
Galleria Akka 056
1-16-20 Higashi-Shinsaibashi
www.g-akka.com
Glico Man sign 015
1 Dotonbori-dori
Graf 073
4-1-9 Nakanoshima
T 06 6459 2100
www.graf-d3.com
Grand Front 072
4-1 Ofukacho
T 06 6372 6300
Granknot 025
1-23-4 Kita-Horie
T 06 6531 6020

H
Hanadori 044
7F Dojima Hotel
2-1-31 Dojimahama
T 06 6341 3042
www.dojima-hotel.com
Hanshin Racecourse 088
1-1 Komano-cho
Takarazuka
Hyogo
www.japanracing.jp
Hep Five 012
5-15 Kakuda-cho
T 06 6313 0501
www.hepfive.jp
Herbis Plaza 072
2-5-25 Umeda
T 06 6343 7500
www.herbis.jp
Hermès 072
3-10-25 Minami-Senba
T 06 4704 7110
www.hermes.com

I
Inujima Seirensho Art Museum 097
327-5 Inujima
Higashi-ku
Okayama
Inujima
T 08 6947 1112
www.benesse-artiste.jp/seirensho

J
Journal Standard 042
1F and 2F E-ma Building
1-12-6 Umeda
T 06 4795 7540
www.journal-standard.jp

K

Kaara 030
  6F Green Terrace Building
  1-1-18 Sonezaki-shinchi
  T 06 6341 2818
Kahala 031
  1-9-2 Sonezaki-shinchi
  T 06 6345 6778
**Kansai International Airport
Terminal** 068
  1 Senshu-kuko Kita
  Izumisano
  T 07 2455 2500
  www.kansai-airport.or.jp

L

Leach Bar 048
  Righa Royal Hotel
  5-3-68 Nakanoshima
  T 06 6448 1121
  www.rihga.com
Live & Bar 11 050
  Midosuji Building
  1-4-5 Nishi-Shinsaibashi
  T 06 6243 0089
  www.onzi-eme.com

M

Maishima Incineration Plant 070
  1-2-48 Hokkoshiratsu
  T 06 6463 4153
Maison Martin Margiela 085
  Norin Kaikan
  2-6-3 Minami-Senba
  T 06 6282 0009
  www.maisonmartinmargiela.com
Mandarake Grandchaos 054
  2-9-22 Nishi-Shinsaibashi
  T 06 6363 7777
  www.mandarake.co.jp

Metro 077
  BF 82 Ebisu Bill
  Simodutumi-cho kawabata
  Marutamachi kudaru
  Sakyo-ku
  Kyoto
  T 07 5752 4765
  www.metro.ne.jp
Miho Museum 100
  300 Tashiro Momodani
  Shigaraki
  Shiga
  T 07 4882 3411
  www.miho.jp
Mill Pour 032
  3-6-1 Minami-Senba
  T 06 6241 1339
Millibar 036
  Artniks Building
  1-12-17 Itachibori
  T 06 6531 7811
  www.artniks.jp/millibar
Mochisho Shizuku 033
  1-17-17 Shinmachi
  T 06 6536 0805
  www.nichigetsumochi.jp
Mole & Hosoi Coffees 043
  3-3-3 Fushimi-machi
  T 06 6232 3616
  www.mole-and-hosoicoffees.com

N

Nagai Stadium 094
  1-1 Nagai Koen
  Higashi-Sumiyoshi-ku
  T 06 6691 2500
  www.nagai-park.jp

Namba Parks 057
2-10-70 Nambanaka
T 06 6644 7100
www.nambaparks.com

National Museum of Art 062
4-2-55 Nakanoshima
T 06 6447 4680
www.nmao.go.jp

National Museum of Ethnology 063
10-1 Senri Banpaku Koen
Suita
T 06 6876 2151
www.minpaku.ac.jp

Ne 089
2F 1-13-21 Kita-Horie
T 06 4395 5634
www.ne-hair.com

Nobiyaka Kenkokan 092
2760-1 Kanaokacho
Kita-ku
Sakai
T 07 2246 5051
www.sakaiwellness.com

Norin Kaikan 085
2-6-3 Minami-Senba
www.osaka-norin.com

O
Organic Building 066
4-7-21 Minami-Senba

Osaka Castle 013
1-1 Osakajo
T 06 6941 3044
www.osakacastle.net

Osaka Museum of History 011
4-1-32 Otemae
T 06 6946 5728
www.mus-his.city.osaka.jp

Osaka Pool 090
Koen Nai
3-1-20 Tanaka
T 06 6571 2010

P
Prefectural Sayamaike Museum 060
2 Ikejirinaka
Osaka Sayama
T 07 2367 8891
www.sayamaikehaku.osakasayama.
osaka.jp

S
Sagan 052
B1 Le Pont De Ciel Building
6-9 Kitahama-Higashi
T 06 6947 0789
www.pont-de-ciel.co.jp

Sakaisuji Club 051
1-15-12 Minami-Senba
T 06 6265 8000
www.sakaisujiclub.com

Seaside Inujima Gallery 097
327-5 Inujima
Higashi-ku
Okayama
Inujima
T 08 6947 1112
www.benesse-artsite.jp/seaside-inujima

**Sencha To Kutsushita Soshite
Yakuso** 085
Norin Kaikan
2-6-3 Minami-Senba
T 070 5438 2016

Ships 042
3F E-ma Building
1-12-6 Umeda
T 06 4795 7528
www.shipsltd.co.jp
Skit 027
2F RE:001
1-21-16 Minami-Horie
T 06 6533 0405
www.skit.cocolog-nifty.com
The Stage 078
3-3-3 Fushimi-machi
T 06 6204 5280
www.kaneko-optical.co.jp
Standard Bookstore 054
2-2-12 Nishi-Shinsaibashi
T 06 6484 2239
www.standardbookstore.com

T
Tarmerry 037
2-4-2 Saiwai-cho
T 06 6567 1130
Toga 076
1-23-7 Kita-Horie
T 06 6533 7538
www.toga.jp
Tokyo Wheels 085
Norin Kaikan
2-6-3 Minami-Senba
T 06 4400 5070
www.tokyowheels.jp
Tower of the Sun 067
1-1 Senri Banpaku Koen
Suita
T 06 6877 7387
www.expo70.or.jp

Truck 080
6-8-48 Shinmori
T 06 6958 7055
www.truck-furniture.co.jp
Tsutenkaku Tower 009
1-18-6 Ebisu-Higashi
T 06 6641 9555

U
Umeda Sky Building 014
1-1-88 Oyodonaka
T 06 6440 3899
www.skybldg.co.jp

W
Wasabi 046
1-1-17 Namba
T 06 6212 6666
www.hozenji-wasabi.jp
Winged Wheel 086
3-6-14 Minami-Senba
T 06 6245 8430
www.winged-wheel.co.jp

Y
Yodoko Guest House 102
3-10 Yamanote-cho
Hyogo
Ashiya
T 07 9738 1720
www.yodoko.co.jp/geihinkan
Yoshino Sushi 040
3-1-14 Awaji-cho
T 06 6231 7181
www.yoshino-sushi.co.jp

HOTELS

ADDRESSES AND ROOM RATES

Dojima Hotel 023
Room rates:
double, from ¥22,000;
Deluxe Room, from ¥30,800;
Junior Suite, from ¥99,000;
Secret Room, from ¥170,000
2-1-31 Dojimahama
T 06 6341 3000
www.dojima-hotel.com

First Cabin 016
Room rates:
double, from ¥5,900
4-2-1 Namba
T 06 6631 8090
www.first-cabin.jp

Hostel 64 018
Room rates:
double, from ¥7,900;
Washitsu Room, from ¥8,100;
Superior Room J-2, from ¥10,500
3-11-20 Shinmachi
T 06 6556 6586
www.hostel64.com

Imperial Hotel 016
Room rates:
double, from ¥32,340
1-8-50 Tenmabashi
T 06 6881 1111
www.imperialhotel.co.jp

Nantenen 016
Room rates:
double, from ¥20,000
158 Amami
Kawachinagano
T 07 2168 8081
www.e-oyu.com

Negiya Ryofukaku 101
Room rates:
double, from ¥135,000;
Rebirth, from ¥415,000
1537-2 Arima-cho
Kita-ku
Hyogo
T 07 8904 0675
www.negiya.jp

The New Otani 016
Room rates:
double, from ¥43,100
1-4-1 Shiromi
T 06 6941 1111
www.newotani.co.jp/osaka

The Ritz-Carlton 017
Room rates:
double, from ¥49,000;
Sky View Deluxe Room, from ¥62,000;
Japanese Suite, from ¥85,000
2-5-25 Umeda
T 06 6343 7000
www.ritzcarlton.com

St Regis 022
Room rates:
double, from ¥62,000;
Grand Deluxe, from ¥67,000;
Grand Deluxe Premier, from ¥67,000
3-6-12 Honmachi-dori
T 06 6258 3333
www.stregisosaka.co.jp

T'Point 020
Room rates:
double, from ¥9,800;
Room 614, from ¥28,000
1-6-28 Higashi-Shinsaibashi
T 06 6251 7170
www.tpoint.co.jp

The Westin 016
 Room rates:
 double, from ¥48,000
 1-1-20 Oyodonaka
 T 06 6440 1111
 www.westin-osaka.co.jp

WALLPAPER* CITY GUIDES

Executive Editor
Rachael Moloney

Authors
Nicholas Coldicott
Gordon Knight

Art Editor
Eriko Shimazaki
Designer
Mayumi Hashimoto
Map Illustrator
Russell Bell

Photography Editor
Elisa Merlo
Assistant Photography Editor
Nabil Butt

Chief Sub-Editor
Nick Mee
Sub-Editor
Farah Shafiq

Editorial Assistant
Emilee Jane Tombs

Interns
Matthew Anstis
Florentyna Leow

Wallpaper* Group
Editor-in-Chief
Tony Chambers
Publishing Director
Gord Ray
Managing Editor
Oliver Adamson

Original Design
Loran Stosskopf

Contributors
Daniel Lee
Chikako Tanaka

Wallpaper* ® is a
registered trademark
of IPC Media Limited

First published 2009
Revised and updated 2014

All prices are correct at
the time of going to press,
but are subject to change.

Printed in China

PHAIDON

Phaidon Press Limited
Regent's Wharf
All Saints Street
London N1 9PA

Phaidon Press Inc
65 Bleecker Street
New York, NY 10012

Phaidon® is a registered
trademark of Phaidon
Press Limited

www.phaidon.com

A CIP Catalogue record for
this book is available from
the British Library.

All rights reserved.
No part of this publication
may be reproduced, stored
in a retrieval system or
transmitted, in any form
or by any means,
electronic, mechanical,
photocopying, recording
or otherwise, without
the prior permission of
Phaidon Press.

© 2009 and 2014
IPC Media Limited

ISBN 978 0 7148 6836 3

PHOTOGRAPHERS

Daici Ano
Inujima Seirensho Art
Museum, p097, pp098-099

Yoshiro Masuda
Osaka city view,
inside front cover
Abeno Harukas, pp010-011
Hostel 64, p018, p019
St Regis, p022
Granknot, p025
Contemporary Art Space
Osaka, pp028-029
Kaara, pp030-031
Mochisho Shizuku, p033
Fukura Suzume,
pp034-035
Brooklyn Roasting
Company, p038, p039
Yoshino Sushi, pp040-041
Mole & Hosoi
Coffees, p043
Wasabi, p046, p047
Leach Bar, pp048-049
Chiaki Kohara, p055
Namba Parks, p057
Asahi Broadcasting
Corporation, pp058-059
Graf, pp074-075
The Stage, pp078-079
Truck, p080, p081

Elttob Tep, pp082-083
Norin Kaikan, p085
Winged Wheel, pp086-087
Ne, p089

Christoffer Rudquist
Hep Five, p012
Osaka Castle, p013
Umeda Sky Building, p014
Glico Man sign, p015
The Ritz-Carlton, p017
Dojima Hotel, p023
D&Department Project,
p026, p027
Millibar, p036
Tarmerry, p037
Café & Books
Bibliothèque, p042
Hanadori, pp044-045
Live & Bar 11, p050
Ambrosia, p051
Sagan, pp052-053
Prefectural Sayamaike
Museum, pp060-061
National Museum
of Art, p062
National Museum of
Ethnology, p063,
pp064-065
Organic Building, p066
Tower of the Sun, p067
Kansai International
Airport Terminal,
pp068-069

Maishima Incineration
Plant, pp070-071
Toga, p076
Especial Records, p077
Calo Bookshop
& Café, p084
Osaka Pool, pp090-091
Nobiyaka Kenkokan,
p092, p093
Nagai Stadium, pp094-095

Daisuke Shimokawa
Negiya Ryofukaku, p101

Yasunori Shimomura
Graf tamo wood
chair, p073

OSAKA
A COLOUR-CODED GUIDE TO THE HOT 'HOODS

MINAMI
Neon-tastic streets and hip hangouts mean Minami is as colourful as it is atmospheric

KITA
Skyscrapers vie to outdo each other in this lively district filled with Osaka's teen tribes

NAKANOSHIMA
Osaka's main financial centre is crisscrossed by two rivers, the Tosabori and the Dojima

OSAKA CASTLE
Ancient meets modern where the city's concrete castle overlooks the business park

THE BAY
The old port has been reinvented as a cultural hub replete with dramatic architecture

TENNOJI
Shitennoji Temple is a major draw, and so is Abeno Harukas, Japan's highest building

For a full description of each neighbourhood, see the Introduction.
Featured venues are colour-coded, according to the district in which they are located.